HEALING WITHIN

Rising to an Empowered life

TANYA GATES

Copyright © 2019 (Tanya Gates)
All rights reserved worldwide.

No part of the book may be copied or changed in any format, sold, or used in a way other than what is outlined in this book, under any circumstances, without the prior written permission of author.

Publisher: Inspiring Publishers,
P.O. Box 159, Calwell, ACT Australia 2905
Email: publishaspg@gmail.com
http://www.inspiringpublishers.com

 A catalogue record for this book is available from the National Library of Australia

National Library of Australia The Prepublication Data Service

Author: Tanya Gates
Title: Healing Within
Genre: Non-fiction
ISBN: 978-1-925908-27-5

I dedicate this book to
my soulmate, best friend and true love,
Ash
whose unconditional love has helped set me free

My Intention

I started writing this book several times,
but it wasn't until I set a clear intention
that the words started flowing.

My intention for writing this book is to help others.
To be open and honest, and to always come from a
place of love. But also, to further my own healing
through writing.

To understand everything is to forgive everything.

-Buddha

Introduction

I decided many years ago how I wanted to live my life. I embrace every day with love, and I take the time to see the beauty in every experience I have: watching a little finch sipping the morning dew off a leaf, hearing the sweet song of a blue wren, feeling the cool air of a native bee's wings as it hovers over me, and taking in the smile and embrace of a child as they wrap their arms around me, sharing their unconditional love.

This is how I choose to live, seeing all the little miracles around me. We can get so caught up in our daily routines that we miss these precious moments.

My hope is that sharing my journey to awakening with you will help you along your journey too.

Pregnancy

My parents' story is one that has been heard many times before. Couple fall in love, girl falls pregnant, an ultimatum is given to the young man by his parents: to leave his love or be cut out of the family inheritance.

My birth father was an only child with land to inherit. My mother was from a working-class family that struggled financially. In the eyes of my birth father's parents, she was not good enough for their son to marry.

My birth father chose the inheritance and left to live in Australia until the time that he would marry and return to take over the family property.

There was a lengthy court battle in which my mum, (still pregnant with me at the time), had to prove that my birth father was in fact my father, even though they had been together in a long-term relationship. In the end, Mum proved that he was my father, and his name was placed on my birth certificate.

Just Us Two

It was just Mum and I until I was nine years old. My memories of those first nine years are happy ones. We never had much money, but I never wanted for anything. Mum would make me these beautiful dresses and skirts in bright colours. I remember laughing and twirling around to music, watching my dress fan out while spinning as fast as I could.

We had this big old black car. Mum would have to sometimes crank start it to get it going. I would be sitting on a pillow on the front seat so I could see out the window, and right next to me would be my little case that I would carry everywhere with all my special things in it. I felt happy, loved and safe.

Mum is the eldest of seven brothers and sisters, so there was always a lot of playing and laughter around me too. One treasured memory I have is with my uncle. He would sit me on the bench and sing the Neil Diamond song 'Tanya' to me. I would sit there glowing with happiness, feeling so special and loved.

GRANDAD GARRITY

I believe that there are people who come into our lives when we need them, either for love or guidance or both. I am lucky enough to have a number of those people who have been with me through this journey—some very briefly, but they have made such a big impact that it has helped me and shaped me into who I am today. I thank them all for what they have taught me and for all the unconditional love they have given me.

I don't really remember how I met Grandad and Granny Garrity, so this story of my first meeting with them is from what my mum has told me, but for as long as I can remember, they have been in my life.

Mum told me Grandad and Granny Garrity used to live down the street from us. One day I decided to venture out by myself with my little fluffy dog, Blue, riding my three-wheeler trike. I was three at the time. They were in the garden, and as I rode my trike past, I stopped and started chatting to them. They figured out where I lived and took me home to Mum. From that moment on, I would always go and see them, and they became my special grandparents and I became their special granddaughter.

I remember when I was at primary school, I would go to their house after school and play the organ for hours. They would ask me how school was going, and Granny would make me cookies. Grandad used to call me Goldilocks. Back then I had long auburn hair, and I loved hearing him call me that. It made me feel very special.

The years went on, and I would always call in and sometimes stay with them. They moved to Chester Road, just out of Carterton. That was only five minutes away from where my future husband was living, if only I had known. To tell the truth, it would have freaked me out to know.

Brother Reg

There was an incident while I was attending primary school in my home town of Carterton where one of the teachers went to hit a boy with a ruler but slipped and got me instead. I went home with a bruise on my arm.

I was removed from my primary school that day and enrolled into Chanel Intermediate College in Masterton, which is a Catholic school. We would go to church on Monday mornings and say prayers before and after class.

In my second year there, my teacher was Brother Reg. He was like a big, gentle giant, tall with bright red hair and a beard. When he laughed, it lit up the room.

He would always listen to me and encourage me to do my best, telling me that I could do anything if I believed in myself. He believed in me, and that meant the world to me. I worked extra hard for Brother Reg. That was the only time I ever received an A for my school work. But after that second year, I was to leave and go to a different high school. I wrote to him on and off for the next year. He was sent to help at a mission somewhere overseas, sadly I lost contact with him.

Dad

Mum married when I was about nine years old. My stepfather (whom I call Dad) adopted me legally. I was so happy to have a dad.

The family began to grow, and within a three-year period, I had two new brothers. I love both my brothers dearly. They are and will always be a part of me, no matter where each of us is living in the world. But I was so used to having Mum all to myself for those first years of my life. The family had grown from just the two of us to five, with two little babies needing a lot of attention.

When my teenage years arrived, the rebelling started. I had a lot of hurt and rejection simmering away under the surface. The more that Dad would yell at me, the more I refused to listen. I dug my heels in, and believe me, I was a stubborn redhead. We clashed on everything and anything.

Things at home got so bad between Dad and I that I was sent to live with my Nana. Deep down, I felt pushed out and unwanted.

Remembering

It was also during this period that my memory was about to be given a jolt. I had just turned fourteen years old. I was being driven home one night after going to the movies in Masterton, and I started to feel uneasy.

It's funny how when the mind and body are traumatised they can block things out until the time comes when the person is strong enough to handle things. That time had come for me.

The car went straight past the turn off to Nana's house. The further away I got from Nana's house, the sicker I felt in my stomach. The driver pulled off the main road and went down a dirt track and then stopped the car. We were at the river.

There was complete silence and then he said, "Do you remember what we used to do?"

I said no, that I felt sick and wanted to go to Nana's. There was silence. It felt like ages went by, and then the car started, and I was driven to Nana's house.

I remember closing the door to my bedroom, sick in my tummy and feeling so alone. I got into bed and hid under the blankets. In that moment when he asked me the question, "Do you remember?" All the memories came flooding back to me from when I was nine years old.

Looking back now, if I could say anything to that young girl, it would be, "You are loved, you are wanted and safe", then I would wrap my arms around her and hold her tight.

A few months later, I went to live back home, but I never told anyone what had happened.

RISING TO AN EMPOWERED LIFE

As I sit in the sunlight,
I feel the warm embrace
Of Mother Nature & this wondrous place.

Violets & daphne filling the air,
An inner peace flowing through,
Replacing despair.

In this present moment,
I have come to understand
That all we need to do is ask &
We'll receive a helping hand.

Lisa and Kay

I don't really remember having a lot of close friends growing up, until I got to high school and met Lisa. I was a bit of a loner before then. I always felt somewhat out of place, like I never belonged anywhere.

I was so nervous on my first day of high school at Kuranui College. I had lost contact with all my old friends and I knew no-one. I stood at the door of the class room that I had been assigned too and didn't know what to do. All the other students looked like they had paired up and were sitting with people they knew. Then a girl across from me smiled and said, "Would you like to sit next to me?" Her name was Lisa, and we became best friends. She loved drawing and we made each other laugh a lot. She lived in the next town over from me.

Lisa asked if I wanted to stay at her place, and I jumped at the chance. I loved staying there. Her family lived in a big old house with heaps of cats. You would be asleep in bed, then you would feel the blankets move, and a cat would snuggle its way down to the bottom of your feet. The whole feel of the home was calm and tranquil.

Lisa's mum, Kay, was so welcoming and warm, and she always made me feel like she wanted me there. Staying most weekends with Lisa and her family became a regular event. I got to see how a family can live together with love, laughter and happiness flowing through the home. Lisa loved art and the outdoors. She had pet frogs, rats and rabbits. At night Lisa fed hedgehogs at the front door with milk, and she still does so to this day. Her home was a wonderland of experiences for me to explore.

Meeting my Birth Father

My birth father was never in the picture when I was growing up. The first meeting I had with him was when I was about thirteen years old. This was arranged by my high school guidance counsellor, Mr Green. He was a lovely man who helped me so much through those years. I would go and talk to him for hours on end.

On the way to meet my birth father, I had many mixed emotions going on inside me. I was so excited and nervous but also very scared that he wouldn't like me. I had so many questions to ask, things to find out.

My mum has beautiful olive skin, brown eyes and dark hair. Me? Well, I'm fair with red hair and freckles. So, looking in the mirror, I never felt that I belonged in the looks department either.

I walked into the café, and there he was, sitting at the table, waiting for me to arrive. I sat across from him, just staring. I couldn't take my eyes of him. When I looked at him, I saw myself.

Happiness engulfed me but those thoughts of *What if he doesn't like me?* and *What if I'm not good enough? Will he want to see me again?* were still playing in my mind the whole time. We sat there talking for about twenty minutes. To be honest, I can't even remember the conversation, but I remember his face as clear as anything.

I took a deep breath and asked, "Can I see you again?" He replied, "Yes." I felt like I was floating on air. The whole way home, I couldn't stop smiling. Happiness shone through every part of me.

A few days later, I rang to ask when we could meet again. He said that it would be best if we didn't see each other again.

My heart shattered into a thousand pieces. Didn't he like me? Wasn't I good enough? I wasn't pretty enough! I cried until I couldn't cry any more. Then I got angry. (Behind all anger is hurt.) In that moment, I unknowingly placed a wall around my heart so that I would never feel that kind of pain again.

Angelic little butterflies
Flying on a summer's breeze,
They glide & shimmer, dance & swirl,
Courting each other with ease

Capturing my imagination,
As I stand there & stare
The miracle of life & creation
And the love in the air.

ASH

By this time, I had decided that all men either leave you or hurt you and cannot be trusted. I was never going to get married or have children, I didn't want to mess my kids up, like I was.

I meet Ash just before my fifteenth birthday. It was our destiny to be together right from the start.

I was up town on a Thursday night with my friend Amy when a car drove past with two guys in it. Amy waved, and the car pulled over. Not wanting any part of this, I hid in one of the shops. Eventually the car drove off.

Then about half an hour later, they drove past again, but this time they stopped in front of where Amy and I were walking. That meant we would have to walk straight pass them. Amy headed right over to the car and started talking to the driver. I hung back and just wanted to disappear somewhere.

The next thing I knew, Amy had gotten in the back seat of the car, so I reluctantly got in too. Then the guy in the front passenger seat took off his leather jacket.

I remember looking at his shoulders and muscles and feeling butterflies in my tummy. He didn't talk, but his friend and my friend were flirting like mad.

I decided that I had had enough and asked to be dropped off. I didn't give my actual address. I just asked to be dropped off at the top of my street and that is where I got out. I remember feeling so much relief when I got out of the car.

A few days later, Amy told me that the guy in the passenger seat wanted to see me again. I wasn't interested and didn't want a boyfriend. Then the following Thursday night, we went to town again. Thursday was the night for late night shopping when the local teenagers would hang out up town.

The same car drove past and then stopped in front of us. Amy walked over and said straight away, "Well, here's my friend, I brought her with me." I was so embarrassed I wanted the earth to swallow me up, especially when he said, "I never said that." I found out later that he was just as embarrassed as me, and that is why he denied wanting to see me again.

We drove to the park. I had by now been introduced to this guy, whose name was Ash. We went and sat on a bench seat and started talking. We talked for hours, about everything and anything. I had never talked to anyone like that before, let alone a boy, but I still didn't give him my last name or my phone number. It was getting late, and I asked to be dropped off at the end of my street again.

Then Saturday came. I was in the garden with Mum when I could hear someone yelling out. I looked over the fence and down the street. There was the same car, with Ash sitting on the bonnet, yelling out my name. I made my excuses to Mum very fast and disappeared inside the house. Mum came in a short while later and asked if I knew those boys. My reply was, "Of course not!"

A week passed, and I decided to go for a walk into town, which was about thirty minutes from where I lived. As a white car drove past, I put out my thumb. It stopped. I looked into the driver's seat and saw that it was Ash. I stood there and stared. What were the chances of Ash being the one that would stop? After my nerves settled down, I asked him about driving down the street and yelling out. He said he wanted to find me, but he didn't know my actual street address. He had hoped that by yelling my name, I would come out and he would find me. Now it seemed that *Fate* had put us together again.

On that car ride to town, I told him my last name. I never gave him my phone number, but I got his.

Approval

I had turned fifteen by now, and I arranged for Ash to meet Grandad and Granny Garrity. I wanted Grandad's approval, not knowing that they had met a year prior. Ash had run out of fuel for his car, and Grandad had given him some to get home. I could tell that Grandad liked Ash when he gave him a firm handshake and said it was nice to see him again.

A few months after their meeting, Ash called me one night after getting home from work. He said there were a lot of cars at Grandad's house, so something must have happened. I phoned Grandad's place. I'm not even sure who I was speaking too, but they said that Grandad had passed away suddenly. My heart broke even more.

I remember sobbing uncontrollably at the funeral. I couldn't stop the tears; they just kept flowing. I still think of him often and hope that he is proud of me. I was blessed the day that he and Grandma came into my life. He was the Grandad that I never had.

The Plan

Ash and I started seeing each other just about every day, but because of my age, Mum tried to slow things down. She wanted to limit our time together to three times a week, which didn't work. I would say that I was going for a walk, but I was really meeting Ash a few streets over from our house. We would sit and talk and make plans for moving in together. In the end, Mum gave up on trying to restrict us from seeing each other.

A few months passed, and Ash moved into an old farmhouse close to his work. Legally in New Zealand, you must be sixteen years old to leave home without your parents' consent. So, I put a plan into action. My younger brother had a bit of a hot temper back then. I had been asking and pleading with Mum to let me move in with Ash, but she always replied, "No, you're too young."

My poor little brother had no idea, but his big sister was about to take advantage of his temper. One afternoon, I started stirring him. I stirred him and stirred him a bit more, until Mum had enough. She yelled, "Will you stop it!"

I yelled back, "Let me leave!"

Her reply was, "Fine!"

I got straight on the phone and rang Ash at work. "You have to come now," I said, "before Mum changes her mind."

Within twenty minutes, Ash was there, I was packed, and we left.

I spread my wings,
I soar & fly,
Exploring the beauty of the sky.

With light & ease
I feel the touch of the caressing breeze.

Limitations do not exist,
Rising high I feel its bliss

Being connected to the divine
In all directions of space & time.

FREEDOM

That first night when I got to the house, I yelled at the top of my lungs. "I'm free!" No one would ever be telling me what to do again. It was about a month before my sixteenth birthday. I was still going to high school and was about to stay the first night with my boyfriend in our new home, and I was so happy.

I had the worst night's sleep. Every time Ash made the slightest movement, I would wake. Sleeping next to someone took months to get used to.

Then there was getting used to living together. One day when Ash came home for lunch, I had cooked spaghetti on toast for him (for the third day in a row). All he said was, "Oh, spaghetti for lunch again." I lost it, and threw the food straight past his head. It hit the wall. From that moment on, he told me that if I didn't want to cook, he wouldn't expect me to.

I always felt like I had a storm going on in my stomach, whirling around. I didn't realise it at the time, but it was all those emotions that I had been pushing down.

Sometimes Ash would say something that would seem harmless to anyone else hearing it, but to me it hit one of those thorns that had lodged there years earlier from pain that I hadn't dealt with. Instead of just getting a response from me to the interaction we were having, he ended up getting all the hurt that I had ever felt fired at him. I was screaming for help with the pain that I was carrying around inside.

We would talk and smooth things over, but I never realised until now, while writing these words, what was happening to me back then. Yes, the healing is happening through the words I am writing. I have tears flowing, but I am also smiling.

I finished my exams and then continued my schooling for another year by correspondence. Ash and I were best friends, and we were growing closer together in every way, talking about childhood stuff and our families. I had told Ash about the sexual abuse I had experienced but, I made him promise not to tell anyone or to confront the person who had done it. He understood it was not his secret to tell and that I wasn't ready yet for anyone to know about it, let alone deal with the emotional pain of it. He would stay true to me and keep my secret for many years, until I was ready. Thank you, Ash.

But there was still always a part of myself that I kept protected. I was still waiting for that day that Ash would leave me.

There were certain things that I just could not do. I could never go up to him for a hug or ask for a kiss. That would mean that I was leaving myself open, and I needed to keep that wall up. I thought that seeking affection meant I was showing weakness, and if I showed weakness, I would get hurt.

At one point in our relationship, not long after we started living together, I told Ash that I needed to experience what it would be like to live on my own. I said I needed to see what it was like, but really, I think I was trying to keep him at arm's length.

When I was sixteen, I moved in with Lisa. We were working together and living together. In our case, it was not the best thing for our friendship. We lived together for a few months, then Lisa and I stopped speaking to each other. I moved back in with Ash.

Married with Children

The years passed, and Ash and I got married just before my eighteenth birthday. We had two beautiful children, Clinton and Chelsea. Even though I had sworn that I would never have children, when they arrived, I loved them to bits. All those beautiful cherished moments of smiles, first laughs, hearing the word "Mum" come from their little mouths. I wouldn't have changed a thing.

Through having children of my own, I also developed a better understanding of my own childhood. I realised that my parents were working through their own stuff. I appreciate now that they did the best they could possibly do at that stage in their lives.

Ash was employed on a dairy farm, working very long hours and most weekends. I was at home with two children and doing relief milking at the weekends to help make ends meet. Ash and I hardly got to see each other. Something had to change.

I was sitting there one evening when the answer came to me. We need to move to Australia. I said to Ash, "I'm going to put an advertisement in the *Australian Dairyfarmer* magazine", and I did. To me it was clear. We needed to go somewhere where our children would have a better chance financially and where Ash and I would get to see more of each other.

Ash wasn't keen on the idea to start with. He always said that he would never leave the Wairarapa, but he agreed in the end. Later he told me he only agreed because he thought no one would reply to the advertisement.

Four weeks later the phone rang. It was a couple from New South Wales in Australia, offering us a share-farming job. The job required both of us to milk, but I only had to milk through calving time. We discussed the offer and decided to go for it. We did not go and have a look at the job in Australia before making our decision because we never had the money for air flights. We had three months to sell everything and be at our new job.

Repairing A Friendship

I had just had both our children's portraits taken, when I glanced across to the bus stop and saw Lisa sitting there waiting for the bus. What was the chance of me bumping into my old friend, who I hadn't seen in a couple of years, and just before I was to head off to Australia?

I didn't have the courage to go and talk to her, so I carried on putting the kids in their car seats. When I looked up, Lisa was standing next to me. She said hello and asked if I would like to come around one night to her parents' house and talk.

Ash watched the kids, and I went to meet Lisa. I was so nervous, but as soon as I got there, she made me feel at home. I had that same old feeling that I used to get when I stayed there: the feeling of warmth and love.

We talked for hours, mostly of high school and all the things we used to get up to, about our dreams and what we had been doing the last couple of years. With every word spoken, our friendship was healing. We both agreed never to let anything come in the way of our friendship again.

Lisa is still one of my best friends today. It's one of those friendships where the two of you may not speak for a few months, but when you do it's like you just spoke only yesterday. A lifetime friend whom I love very much. I give a big thank you to the heavens for bringing us back together.

RISING TO AN EMPOWERED LIFE

So tiny & brave & without any fear,
They release their silk & float into the air.

Where will they be carried? They do not know.
Without any hesitation they just let go.

So thank you, little spider, for sharing with me
That following my instincts will always set me free.

Australia

We arrived in Australia in 1993 with two small children, our love for each other, and a dream for the future. Failing never even entered my mind, thanks to Brother Reg.

I was full of excitement and wonder about what was ahead. When we arrived at the airport, we were picked up by our new boss. We stayed with them for the first night. As I lay in bed, I wondered what I had done. I was in a strange country and I felt homesick for New Zealand. After a while, I drifted off to sleep.

The next morning the excitement kicked in again. We borrowed our boss's car and drove to Swan Hill to buy furniture for the house that came with the job. It was a major learning curve for us.

Those first few months were hard. Some days, the temperature got up to 47 degrees. Back where we lived in New Zealand, it got to 29 degrees if you were lucky. To top things off, there was a mouse plague! Our first job in Australia was not going to plan. We left that position after ten months.

During the time we had been in the area, we had met a lovely family who owned a large rice farm. They offered us a house rent-free if Ash would help out now and then.

A Fresh Start

Here we were in Australia, with no jobs, not much money left, and living in the middle of nowhere. We decided that if we did not get a job offer after a few months of not working, we would head back to New Zealand and start again.

Within a week of deciding this, a message was passed on to us to call a farmer in Koondrook. He had a 200-cow dairy farm and was wanting to employ us. We arranged to meet. It turned out that a representative from a herd improvement company had seen the calves that Ash had raised in our previous job and had said they were the best raised calves he had seen in a while.

The two drawbacks with the job were that we would be living right next to the Gunbower Creek, which was only ten feet from our front door, and I had to milk all season. We said that a pool fence would have to be put up around the house for the children before we would move in. We also decided to employ someone from New Zealand to be the second milker, giving someone else the opportunity to come over to Australia and have a fresh start like we did. That person ended up being Bryce, who still lives in Australia to this day.

The area that we lived in had a great community feel, with many events going on for the kids. The people were very friendly and welcoming, but we soon realised that we weren't getting anywhere financially. It was costing a lot to employ someone when I could do the job myself. I had put on a lot of weight by this point, partly from being pregnant, but I was also eating to block my feelings. I eat to feel better, craving that sugar high, but then I would crash and feel even worse. I always had trouble expressing my emotions. It was like the words would get stuck in my throat, and after a while I would explode by yelling. Or, I would just eat.

I thought that working would keep me busy and help get the weight off, and it did. I was milking morning and night, taking care of two children, and studying in between. I decided that in order to manage our finances properly, I had to learn. I enrolled in a business management course and learnt how to use a computer.

Meanwhile, Ash was flat out working on the farm. One of the things that we loved about farming was that we could see each other throughout the day.

Ignoring my Health

I have a tendency to take things to extremes. When I started losing weight, I loved seeing the number on the scales get lower each week. Then I started weighing myself every day. I started eating just two meals a day, and then the portion sizes got smaller and smaller.

Ash started commenting how my ribs were sticking out, but I just laughed it off. When I looked in the mirror, I never saw ribs or a flat stomach. I saw the weight I was when I was at my biggest. I remember sitting and watching someone eat, and in my head, I was hearing, *I'm so proud of you for not eating.* By this point I had lost 36 kilograms.

I got the flu, which I had had before. No big deal, but it wouldn't go away. I didn't go to the doctor, and I was still exercising because I was worried that if I stopped, I would gain weight again.

I just ignored the hot sweats and the trouble I was having breathing. All I could think was that I needed to keep exercising. I remember lying on the bed one day. The kids were at school, and I was gasping for breath.

Loud and clear I heard, *Go to the doctor.* I made an appointment for a few hours later, arranged for Ash to do the milking on his own, and took the kids with me.

The doctor took my blood pressure, checked my chest and temperature, and then he picked up the phone and called the hospital, saying, "There's a young woman on her way whom I am admitting."

I spent eight nights in hospital. My temperature skyrocketed, and I was delirious for the first two nights, waking with sweat dripping off me. The nurses had to bathe me and help dress me again. After that, I had to spend two months sleeping in the lounge room with the fire going to help the pneumonia heal.

Looking back, I know why I went to the extremes that I did. I was always the biggest one in my class. My aunties were all thin and pretty. Growing up, I always wanted to be like them. I remember one of aunties saying, "You need to stop growing or you won't fit into my clothes anymore." She didn't mean anything harmful by it, but I took it as her telling me I was getting fat. Then there was also my birth father's rejection, when he said he did not want to see me again. In my mind, it was because I wasn't pretty enough.

So, when I started losing the weight and looking good on the outside, I thought that I was going to feel great on the inside too. I soon discovered that it doesn't work like that.

The Decision

The winter before we were to move jobs again, we decided to go to New Zealand for a holiday, but also to decide where we were going to live permanently. Both our children had started primary school and were settled, so we didn't want to be constantly moving them.

Ash and I said to each other that when we got on the plane to fly back to Australia, we'd both say at the same time where we want to live: Australia or New Zealand. We spent four weeks in New Zealand, but it was different this time. I felt like I had outgrown the life that I once had there. It was the same place, but I was totally different. Ash and I were so much more strongly bonded now. In Australia we only had each other. There was no one else to interfere or help; just the two of us to work through things. Our family unit was very tight, with Ash, me, and our two beautiful children.

At the end of our time in New Zealand we sat on the plane, looked at each other, and both said at the same time, "Australia." New Zealand was no longer home for us.

The original plan when we first came to Australia was to only be here for four years. We'd make our fortune, then go back to New Zealand. I remember just before I left to live in Australia, I gave my Nana a hug goodbye and said, "It's okay, Nana. It's just for a few years."

She looked at me and said, "You're not coming back to New Zealand to live again." She was so matter-of-fact about it that I stood there looking at her.

Turns out you were right, Nana.

Healing Within

As I sit in stillness,
I am totally aware
Of nature's beauty everywhere.

I hear the sweet song
Of a little blue wren,
Its beautiful notes so calming & zen.

Mother Nature gives so much
With her never-ending, magical touch.

Starting to Heal

While on the trip to New Zealand, I had decided to make a call to my birth father. I was nervous to say the least. As I picked up the phone, my hands were shaking. My thought was, *I'll call him. It's either going to be yes or no to meet again.*

The phone rang, and I got the answering machine. To be honest, it was a big relief. I gave the date when I was flying back to Australia. I also gave him the phone number where I was staying and said that if he wanted to see me, he could reach me there. Then I hung up, in shock, wondering if I had just done the right thing. In the back of my mind I was thinking he wouldn't call, but in my heart, I was hoping he would.

The next day, the phone rang, and it was my birth father. He wanted to see me and asked if I would like to bring Ash and the children. That helped my nerves. Ash was my rock, my support system, my everything. I really don't think that I could have gone to meet my birth father if Ash wasn't there with me. Thank you, Ash.

We arrived at the farm and were welcomed by my birth father and his wife. We sat at a large table while the kids were outside playing. I finally had the opportunity to ask every question that had ever haunted me, every question that I had carried around for all those years.

We spoke for hours, and the tears just kept on flowing until I didn't think I could cry any more, but more tears came, clearing out so much old pain and hurt.

I am thankful every day that that meeting happened, because it started my healing within.

Throughout the years that followed, there have been many more visits and conversations with my birth father. I remember one time while I was staying at my birth father's house, we were sitting around the fire one evening, when he reached over and touched my foot in a gesture of love. It was a simple and beautiful thing for a father to express to his daughter, but in that moment, I felt shock and unease within myself.

Looking back now I realise that while growing up, I never had that kind of affection from a male figure in my life. So, when this simple but beautiful moment happened, instead of feeling happiness, I felt uncertainty about what to do and how to feel.

While writing this, I'm feeling a sadness arise in me for that young girl and for how scared and unsure she was back then.

The Interview

Back in Australia, as the years went on, it became clear that the owner of the farm where we were working was coming to the end of his dairy farming days. He didn't want to advance things on the farm but was happy to just plod along. In contrast, there was Ash and I, raring to go, to learn, to improve and expand. We didn't fit in there anymore; we had outgrown that farm. So, we started looking through the newspaper for other share-farming jobs.

The first one that caught our eye was a 400-head dairy farm at Marlo in East Gippsland, but we decided to take a second interview at Maffra too. I knew we could do both jobs. We worked well as a team. I had learnt a lot about the business side of things, and I was keen to keep learning. Ash was amazing with animals and knew how to run a farm. I knew without a doubt that we could make it work.

We also wanted to get away from the extreme heat in summer and the cold in winter. We wanted a climate that was more like where we used to live in New Zealand. We had had a holiday in East Gippsland a few years earlier and had loved the area.

We arrived at the first job interview at Maffra. As we did not have any family members to babysit for us, the kids came too. We had the conversation with them about being well behaved. When we got to the interview, the kids went and played in the playroom. The doors were shut while we were talking with the owners of the farm. One of the questions we were asked was about the children: "How well behaved are they while you milk?" My reply was that they were very well behaved, and we had never had any issues.

The owners smiled, and then they opened the doors to the playroom. There were our two children, grinning widely and covered in baby powder from head to toe. The whole room was coated white.

Back in the car, we looked at the kids and laughed. I didn't think we were going to get that job, and we didn't. The way I look at it now is that we were never meant to have that job because we wouldn't have ended up where we are now.

Before we arrived at the next interview, we said to the kids, "Be on your best behaviour, and we'll take you to the toy shop and you can get whatever you want." Yes, we bribed the kids.

On the drive to the interview, I remember looking out the window at the flat paddocks and the rolling hills, smiling at how beautiful it was. The farm was also close to the beach, and I love the beach. I hadn't lived by clear running water in five years since we moved to Australia, so living beside the Snowy River was a dream.

We met the owners and the interview went well—no baby powder in sight. And yes, we took the kids to the toy shop.

After two days, there was no phone call to say if we had gotten the job. Eventually, I decided to call. The voice on the other end of the phone said, "We've been waiting to hear from you both to see if you wanted it."

The next chapter in our lives was about to begin.

MARLO

We moved to Marlo just after the flood hit in 1997. There was silt everywhere, perfect for growing grass, and we had a great first season. The place where we were working was called the show farm of the district. It was one of the biggest dairy farms in the area at that stage.

There was a feeling of needing to keep up appearances. I was at a healthy weight, going to the gym four times a week and still doing the treadmill and every fad diet to maintain my weight and not put anything back on. At that stage in my life, it was all about how I looked. I still wasn't feeling great on the inside, but it was the outside that mattered, wasn't it? Well, that's what I thought back then. I had nice clothes, jewellery and a fast car. Everything looked great, but the pain on the inside was hidden away.

The way I used to make myself feel good was to have a drink on a Friday and Saturday night, and maybe even a joint to mellow me out on the inside and help me socialise. I remember going to dinners and thinking that no one really knew who I was. How could they? I never let them know me. They just knew the pretend me, the me that I wanted them to see. I was so scared of being rejected and not liked that it ruled my life.

I loved Ash dearly, but I was still keeping a safe distance from him, always keeping that harder exterior. I only wanted the two children then, because I knew that I would be able to look after two easier than three on my own. I was still preparing myself for the day that Ash would see the true me and leave. I even went to the extent of having money set aside for when the time came, because every male figure whom I had loved had left me eventually.

I remember going through baby clothes in tears because deep down I had a yearning for another child, but instead I threw myself into more study. I completed a diploma in rural business management and kept on exercising.

I walked upon the earth this morning
In an awakened dream like state,
Taking in the present moment I did not hesitate,
With open eyes & an open heart
Mystified by nature's work of art.

Spun silk draped across the trees
With the sound of humming native bees.
Morning mist dances & sways
As the sun touches with its warming rays.

I wish you all an experience like this,
For this connection with nature is absolute bliss.

Our Own Farm

In our fifth year of sharefarming at Marlo, we went for a car ride with the one and only John Smith. (He's a right character!) He took us for a drive to the Cabbage Tree Creek Falls and on the way home, he said he wanted to take us through this farm he knew of.

As soon as we got to the gateway of the farm, both Ash and I felt butterflies. It was hill country, flats with fresh running creeks through the property. It took our breath away. We looked at each other and knew this was where we wanted to live.

We had been saving money from our sharefarming job for years now, so we had a nice little nest egg. The farm wasn't on the market, but we rang the owners and asked if they would sell. It was a beef farm at that stage.

The owners said that they were planning on listing the property for sale in the spring. They gave us a price, but it was too much for us.

We mentioned the property to the people we were sharefarming for. They said they were looking for a run-off block for their dairy cattle, so Ash and I bought two of the titles and they bought the third title.

We had our farm, our piece of paradise, totally surrounded by bush and nature.

We were still sharefarming and living at Marlo, but we also had our own beef farm at Cabbage Tree Creek. The highlight of our day was going to our farm after we'd finished milking and dreaming of the day when we could stay there forever.

Starting to Trust

By now, that feeling of wanting another child was so strong that it started overwhelming me, to the point where I could not ignore it anymore. I kept on hearing the words in my head: *Will you regret this in ten years' time, if you don't have another child?* The answer was always yes.

I'm not sure if it was the buying of the farm or something else, but on one trip to our farm when the kids were at school, I yelled out to Ash to stop. He pulled over and asked what was wrong.

"I need another baby," I said. He stared at me in a bit of shock then said okay.

To have that third child was a major step for me. I was slowly letting Ash in. I let go of the safety net of the money that I had been putting away. Little by little, the wall was coming down.

Our Baby

We never had a honeymoon when we got married in New Zealand, so we decided that we would have one now. We had family coming over to visit from New Zealand, and they offered to look after the kids while Ash and I went away.

We had a wonderful time away at the Whitsundays with their white sands and calming ocean waters. The whole time we were there, I couldn't shake the feeling that I was pregnant. When we got home, I did a pregnancy test. It turned out I was right: we were pregnant. I was scared but so excited and happy.

A few months passed and then I noticed some spotting. We went to the doctor, and she did a scan that showed we had lost the baby. The doctor told me that they had a free appointment that afternoon at the hospital in Bairnsdale or I would have to wait three days for a curettage. I couldn't bear the thought of carrying the baby that I had lost inside me for three days, so I accepted the appointment for that afternoon. I remember crying while they put me under anaesthetic. I was still crying when I woke up, aching for our baby that I had just lost.

I decided that I must have done something wrong or maybe I was not meant to have another child. I did a few more courses and kept on exercising, trying to forget.

The Clairvoyant

One day I noticed an ad in our local paper for a clairvoyant reading in the town of Newmerella. I rang and made an appointment. I remember when I arrived, there was this little white church in the middle of this paddock. It just looked so out of place.

I was so nervous, I had butterflies in my stomach. I had never done anything like this before. A man greeted me as I walked inside the church. I cannot even remember his name, but he made me feel at ease straight away. I had decided beforehand that I wouldn't say a word about myself, I'd just let him do the talking. I suppose I was a bit sceptical about the whole thing.

"Well, this is strange," he said as he read my cards. It's like you and your husband never asked each other to get married." It was true, but there is no way that he could have known that. I had been about five months pregnant with our eldest child when Mum suggested that Ash and I get married before the baby was born. Ash and I looked at each other and said, "Why not?"

The clairvoyant looked straight at me and said, "You recently lost a child." He looked to his left, like he was listening to someone. I was in a bit of shock. Then he said, "The child is still waiting here to be born." I started crying uncontrollably, letting go of pain that needed to be released. The reading went on for an hour. It was an amazing experience and a healing one for me.

Not long after that, I fell pregnant again. I had a healthy baby boy, weighing eleven pounds (five kilograms). He was one of the biggest babies who had been born in the Bairnsdale Hospital in a while. I had been so worried that I would lose this baby that I just ate my way through the pregnancy and incubated him. I called him my Chocolate Baby, because that's what I lived on through the pregnancy.

I don't look at it like I lost a baby now. The baby that was meant to be born the first time arrived the second time around. We named him Corey.

As darkness is falling,
I hear the night calling,
Whispering softly my name.

What a magnificent sight
I get to see this night!

Such beauty & grace
As I watch the heavens embrace,
Sharing with me all their glory.

Our Adventure

After being at our sharefarming job for almost six years, we handed in our notice. It was time to move to our farm. The first night we stayed there was amazing. We found it hard to go to sleep, we were so happy. It felt like a dream come true. The feeling of waking up in our own home and not having to answer to anyone was absolute bliss.

There were a lot of changes to get used to, though. While working at Marlo, we had a milk cheque once a month, but it came at a price. We had little privacy, a big workload and a lot of stress. We were totally burnt out from our time there, so we welcomed the quieter pace on our new farm with some relief. We didn't care that our monthly milk cheque was going to be replaced with a yearly one. The trade-off was an increase in our privacy and sanity, which meant far more to us.

With our change in circumstances, leaving dairy farming for beef, the bank had given us one month to change banks or they were going to foreclose on the farm. Could our dreams be shattered before we had even really started our new adventure?

We had tried other banks, but we always came up short for them to take us on. It was a stressful time to say the least. After exhausting every avenue to find the extra money we needed, I had given up. Then the phone rang. It was Lisa's mum, Kay. Lisa had filled her in on what was happening in my life. Kay told me to trust and believe. The way was there; I just hadn't found it yet. Her pep talk gave me what I needed to keep going. Thank you, Kay!

A few days later, our rates notice for the farm arrived in the mail. The valuation on the notice had increased to the exact amount that we needed to be able to change banks. We changed banks, and our dream continued.

However we soon realised though that we needed off-farm income to supplement the money coming in from our beef farm. Ash started managing a dairy farm just out of Orbost and travelled there every day while I ran our beef farm. We did this for a few years until we decided it wasn't working for either of us. We were back in the same old circumstances, where we never got to see each other, and the children hardly got to see Ash because he was working such long hours. There needed to be a change.

This time the solution was Ash's idea. He suggested that we convert our beef farm to a dairy farm. If he was going to be milking cows, he'd rather milk his own. We put a proposal together for the bank to convert the farm to a dairy farm. It was approved within a few days.

The Accident

Midway through getting the cowshed built, Ash was fencing one day with a post-hole banger (a weight that gets dropped on top of the post, with two pulleys either side to help bang it in). The cable broke, and the weight came down on Ash's head.

He was airlifted to a hospital in Melbourne, where he had scans and tests. He had a cut on his head and a concussion, but he was okay. The doctor said that he shouldn't have been able to walk away from the accident, but he had, and Ash made a full recovery. The cowshed was finished, thanks to an amazing group of people who helped us build it, and we started milking in the autumn.

Our lifestyle had gone to a faster pace again, but we were okay with that. It was our own farm, and we could be together. Within a year of having the cowshed up and running, our old boss had put the other title to the farm up for sale. We purchased it, and our farm was complete.

By this stage, our eldest son, Clinton, had left home and was studying back in New Zealand. Chelsea was in her final years at high school, and Corey was just about to start school. The days, months and years seemed to be flying by.

Ecstasy

The first time I tried ecstasy, known as the 'love drug', I remember feeling so happy with life, so loving to the world. I had never experienced anything like it before. While taking it that first time, I had a realisation that I had been pushing Ash away for years and keeping him at a distance. For the first time in my life, I walked over to Ash and told him how much I loved him and how sorry I was for withholding myself from him.

After that experience, I researched more about ecstasy and found documentation that it had been used to help release repressed feelings. In learning this, I gave myself the okay to take it again.

I never really looked at it like I was taking a drug. In my mind, I was having therapy on a Friday or Saturday night. That is the excuse that I used to take it, as it allowed me to feel that sensation of openness and love, even if only for a short period of time.

I never realised back then that I could feel open and loving without taking drugs, that all I needed to do was to heal the pain I was holding inside. But to do this, I first had to allow myself to feel the pain and stop blocking it. This realisation would come to me in the years that followed.

To see & be open,
To listen & feel,
To trust & believe
In the wonders & beauty of this world

To feel this moment so fully
That you expand with love

No words could ever fully describe
The happiness & inner peace that is felt inside.

Renewing Our Vows

It was New Year's Eve. Chelsea was still living at home, and Corey was sound asleep in bed. Ash stood before me, then he knelt on one knee and reached for my hand. I hesitated for a moment because I thought something was wrong with him. He looked up at me with a tear in his eye and then asked me to marry him.

I stood there, staring at him in shock. He asked again, "Will you marry me?" This time I answered, "Of course I will!"

To have Chelsea there to share that moment with us was pretty amazing too. She got to watch her father propose to her mother. We all hugged and cried happy tears.

Ash said that he wanted me to have the wedding that I had always dreamed of, so over the next six months the planning and preparations took place. We decided to take a two-week holiday and renew our vows at the end of the first week. We knew with the age of the kids that this was probably going to be our last family holiday together, so we made it a special one.

I remember Chelsea looking at me before the wedding and asking me why I was so nervous when I was already married to her dad, but this time felt so different. Those butterflies had returned once again but this time they were happy nervous butterflies. I was excited but also a bit scared. To me, this was the first time that I was getting married, and I was marrying an amazing, kind-hearted and loving man to whom I had finally opened my heart. It felt so right and so very special this time. Even now while I'm writing this, I'm feeling butterflies in my tummy. Butterflies of love.

We renewed our wedding vows on a secluded beach at Thala Beach Nature Reserve in Port Douglas, Queensland. Clinton walked me to Ash while our song played: 'You're Still the One' by Shania Twain. It fitted us to a T. Chelsea was my bridesmaid, and Corey was the ring bearer. Corey walked to Ash first, carrying a little white pillow with the rings attached. It was just the five of us, our beautiful family unit that we had built together.

Everything was perfect. The wedding vows were romantic and intimate, our children there with us, witnessing their parents' love for each other. We even had the most beautiful sunset. I wore a strapless wedding dress. Ash, Corey, and Clinton wore white linen pants with light blue linen shirts, and Chelsea wore a light blue dress. We were all barefoot on the sandy beach.

After the wedding vows and photographs, we shared a meal together at the treetop restaurant. It was a perfect evening, filled with love and laughter and many beautiful moments. I remember going to the restroom and looking at myself in the mirror. I was filled with so much love and happiness. I twirled around in my wedding dress, like the little girl I once was. I didn't want this magical night to end.

After the meal, Clinton and Chelsea took Corey back to the resort where we had been staying, while Ash and I stayed the night at Thala Beach Lodge. We opened the door to our room, and there were candles lit everywhere. It was so romantic. Unknown to us, Chelsea had snuck away with the manager of the lodge to organise this final, beautiful surprise.

We were nestled in our room amongst the trees as the waves of the ocean serenaded us with their hypnotic sounds. I could not have asked for anything more. It was perfect in every way.

The renewal of our vows signified a new start for us in our relationship. It was also a letting go of the past.

Time for A Change

It felt like things were changing fast inside me now. The more I spoke about things, the more I was clearing out all the old hurt, and the more my life changed. In a conversation with Mum, I at last told her about the sexual abuse that had happened to me when I was younger. To actually speak of it out loud to her and not hide it anymore or keep it a secret was scary but life-changing. When I spoke those words, it was like my throat opened and something was released.

Both Clinton and Chelsea had left home by now and were spreading their wings, finding their own paths.

It's funny how certain events have a way of changing your perspective on things. That is what happened to me. We went through a crisis that shook our whole family unit. That is not my story to tell, but I decided at this point that I needed to make another change. I stopped drinking, smoking pot and taking ecstasy.

A Turning Point

While I was away on a holiday in New South Wales, I decided to get a massage. I walked into this little shop down a side alley. I'm not even sure how I found it. I was given a sheet with a description of all the different types of massages available. I saw one listed as a reiki healing and asked what it was. It was explained to me that reiki helps to remove any energetic blockages in the chakras. I booked in for a reiki healing.

Halfway through the healing, while the reiki practitioner was healing my heart chakra, I burst into tears. She assured me that this was normal and part of the healing; just a release of blocked energy. When I went to leave, the reiki practitioner gave me a crystal. That was my first real introduction to reiki, energy and crystals. The experience had a lasting effect, though, in a wonderful way.

On the way back to where I was staying, I passed a little bookshop. I walked in and went straight over to a book that seemed to stand out to me. It was all about the chakras and energy, and it explained what energy healing was in full detail. I bought it and read the book from cover to cover in two days.

From there, I did an online course in metaphysical studies. I also started doing guided meditations that I had downloaded onto my iPod. Before long, my day consisted of studying the course, practising meditation and reading spiritual texts. I absorbed myself in all things spiritual, to the point that I suppose you could say that I removed myself from my old way of life. That old life didn't fit me anymore.

When I started making changes to my life, it wasn't just the drinking and recreational drug use that changed. It was also what I ate. I became vegan, and I changed the music I listened to. I also found that I didn't want to watch television much. I formed a love for crystals too. Everything I was doing, all the changes I was making, felt so right to me.

All these changes I was going through, meant that my relationship with Ash also changed. Ash hardly recognised this new person who was his wife, and he couldn't understand the new way I wanted to live. For a while, it was like I was living a double life. There was the old me, the one that Ash was trying to hold onto even though she no longer existed, and the new me that was emerging and spreading her wings.

RISING TO AN EMPOWERED LIFE

I step out of the shadows & into the light,
For the first time in my life, I have clear sight.

I open my heart & let go of the fear,
Healing any hurt that still might be there.

Throughout this lifetime, I have come to understand
That angels are always there to give us a helping hand.

Clear Sight

It was like I had woken from a deep sleep and things were totally different. I was totally different. The colours were brighter, and I was feeling everything so much more. I felt new somehow. I started seeing things more vividly too, like colors around people. When someone was angry, I would see a grey or black fog around them.

I was more than a bit freaked out at this stage. I couldn't tell Ash what I was seeing and experiencing. He would think I was nuts. I kept what was happening to myself because I was so worried about what people would think. I absorbed myself even further into spiritual reading and tried to learn more about what I was experiencing.

Another thing that happened is that I started feeling other people's emotions, although at the time I never realised it was their emotions that I was feeling. I was confused and thought that maybe I *was* going nuts. I felt better when I was by myself, so that is what I did. I pulled myself away from everyone.

I started bushwalking and spending hours in the bush, which helped me keep things together. I discovered a love for photographing nature, and I started writing poetry. Words would just flow through me, describing how I was feeling and all the beauty I was seeing. Everything in nature looked so beautiful to me. I am so grateful that I started bushwalking because it has helped me and healed me so much.

Rebuilding

The more I distanced myself from Ash, the more he would try to talk to me. Whenever he got upset, all I saw was the grey and black around him. I would physically feel what he was feeling and visually see his emotional energy. Whenever that happened, I wanted to get out of there as fast as I could, back to the bush where I felt good and saw beautiful things. The more I experienced this, the more I distanced myself from him. I felt disconnected and alone, like I didn't belong. What was I going to say: "Hey, I'm seeing colours and feeling all your emotions"?

A point came in our relationship when something had to change. The more Ash got upset and worried about us as a couple, the more I felt that he didn't love me for who I was now. He was trying to turn the clock back to the way things were, but I couldn't even remember who or how I once was. The old me was gone.

We were so disconnected from each other. I kept on hearing the words, *You need to leave. You need to leave.*

But I knew with all my heart and soul that I loved Ash. How could things be turning out like this? After all these years, I had finally let him in, and now we were falling apart. I couldn't believe it was ending like this.

The moment that things changed for me was at the beach. We had another disagreement, and words came out of my mouth that I never thought I would hear: "If you can't accept me for the way I am now, I have no choice but to leave."

I had no idea at the time, but my relationship was undergoing a major shift. It was getting rebuilt.

I was reading a book the other day, *Light is the New Black*, written by Rebecca Campbell. One sentence I read rang so true for me: "The relationships that are meant to last will adapt to the change in energy."

For Ash and me to stay together, there had to be a change. I had to have the freedom to expand and grow. From that point on, things seemed to settle and begin to change, but there was still a distance between us.

By now I had figured out that I was actually seeing other people's auras and feeling other people's emotions. It was a big relief for me to finally understand and know that what I was feeling was their energy and not mine.

I kept meditating. I didn't need the guided meditations anymore; I was confident enough to meditate by myself. Meditation helps me to centre and ground myself, and this in turn helps me to recognise what is my energy and what is not.

I started having people come into my life who could help me with what was happening with me on an energetic level. I started going to yoga and went on a yoga retreat one weekend. It came up in conversation that I would love to learn reiki, and before I knew it, I was booked into learn reiki shortly after the retreat.

You don't see it at the time, but when you take a good look back, you can actually see the synchronicity in events that happen and that have led you along the path to where you are now.

I became a reiki practitioner and absolutely loved it. But I soon realised that I still had a lot of healing to do myself first before I could help others. I was taking on my clients' energy and pain during the healings, so I decided to stop for a while and work on totally healing myself!

Seeing the Light

Each day there was something new for me to work through. I was learning to let go, move forward, and trust in what was happening in my life. In doing so, I was feeling more at peace with what I was experiencing.

Ash started asking me questions over a period of time. I spoke honestly to him and started opening up and explaining why I believe the things I do and why I want to live the way I do. Slowly but surely, he was getting to know me, and I was opening up this side of myself to him that I had previously shut him out of.

We were sitting outside one sunny morning, having a cuppa and talking, when I hesitated in what I was about to say. Ash reassured me that I could tell him anything and that after everything that we had gone through, we were destined to stay together.

I took a deep breath and told him about being able to physically feel and visually see other people's emotions on an energetic level.

He sat there, listening to every word I was saying. I told him what I could see when we disagreed. I told him everything. He took it all in, then he told me how much sense it all made now, about the way I would react when he tried to talk to me. He thanked me for trusting him enough to be honest and open, and said that he was so sorry that I had to go through all of this alone. I burst into tears. I felt total relief and knew that from now on, I could let Ash into every part of me.

Not Listening

A few years ago, I received a phone call from my dear friend Lisa, telling me her mum was sick. I decided to go to New Zealand and be with her to help. I went to book the flight to New Zealand and kept hearing, *Thirtieth. Book the thirtieth.* I asked about it, but the flights on that date were more expensive, so I ignored the voice in my head and booked a cheaper flight and waited. The morning after I arrived in New Zealand, Lisa's mum passed away, and I never got to see her or hug her. I felt guilty about that for a very long time. Why had I not listened and booked a flight on the thirtieth? If I had done that, I could have seen her. I just wasn't listening and trusting, that's all there is to it.

It has taken me a long time to forgive myself for not seeing Kay before she passed away, but I know in my heart she hears me and knows how much I loved her.

I went and saw her at the house when the family were mourning her. I asked for help to stay strong and hold it together before I walked into the room. This was the first time that I had ever seen anyone in an open casket who had passed away. She looked so peaceful and frail. I stood before her and wept, and as I wept, I felt a blanket of warmth wrap around me like a hug, letting me know it was okay and that Kay knew I was there. She was like a second mum to me, and I cherish all that she shared with me. Thank you, Kay. For everything.

The sun on my back,
Soil beneath my feet,
My connection with the earth is complete.

The wind blows gently through the trees,
Leaves fall, cascading down with ease.

Delicate scents fill the air,
Mother Nature's aroma is everywhere.

Native flowers with colours so bright,
Each time I'm here it feels just right.

Healing Within

Throughout all those hours I spent in the bush, so much healing happened within me. I was able to watch all the thoughts and emotions that were going on inside. By releasing all that old pain, I slowly began to heal.

Through this period in my life, I had so many realisations about why I did the things I did, and why I wouldn't do certain things; why I feel the way I do in certain situations or when people say certain things to me.

Each time I had a realisation about something, I would feel the release inside. The tears would flow, and the healing would happen. At one point I cried almost every day for months. It was intense! But each time I had a release of energy from held emotions, I would feel a little bit better inside myself.

It was through this time that I realised that I had been holding onto guilt. While I was growing up, I would get told stories about what Mum had gone through to keep me. I know that Mum did not tell me these things in order to cause guilt in me in anyway, but to a young child, it weighed heavily. I felt guilty for making her life so hard. If she hadn't fallen pregnant with me or made the decision to keep me, things wouldn't have been so hard for her.

I even went to the extreme in my late twenties of getting the original documents from the court case between my parents. I would read them repeatedly, and each time I did, it was like I was punishing myself.

Ash asked me one evening, "Why do you read them when it makes you upset?" I couldn't answer him. I realised that I needed to let it go, so that night we lit a fire outside. With Ash and Chelsea's help, I burnt the documents. While doing this, I burst into tears. I felt a release of energy and the sensation of being lighter in myself.

I have always had abandonment issues. Realising this also has helped me to heal. Sometimes I still have these emotions arise, but the difference now is that I am aware of them.

Looking back, I can see that Dad taught me strength. Because of my relationship with him and how we were through my teenage years, I developed an inner strength and determination not to give up. Now when I go to visit him in New Zealand, Dad gives me a big hug and always has tears in his eyes. He has a big heart, and I love him dearly.

I learnt how to forgive myself as well as others, for if I cannot forgive myself, how can I forgive someone else? There have been many things throughout my lifetime that I wish I could change, but I cannot change the past; I can only learn from it, and in learning from it changes my future.

I have also forgiven the person who sexually abused me–not for them, but for myself. For so many years, I carried around guilt and shame over that experience.

Throughout this period of healing in my life, the sexual abuse would come up constantly, vividly, like I was reliving it. I wrote a letter to the person in my journal. I told them how much pain they had caused me, and not just me, but that the hurt had carried through to my relationship with Ash. Then I burnt the letter and asked for help in forgiving them and help for me to heal. Over a period of time, it happened. I no longer have the chains that used to way me down.

To this day, I still have moments where I have realizations and a release of emotions. Every time this happens, it feels like I have more space inside me and I'm a bit lighter. I embrace the healing process that is happening in my life.

The healing that has happened within me has been intense, but I would not change a thing. I am so grateful for all my prayers that were heard, and that when I asked for divine help, I always received it.

I also make sure that I take the time to appreciate how far I have come on this journey. I look at all the healing that has happened, and I appreciate all the help that I have received along the way.

I dance & frolic amongst the trees,
Embracing each moment with a peaceful ease,
Not thinking of the future or past
But being fully present in this moment at last.

The lessons that I have learnt along the way
Have shaped me into whom I am today.
So, thanks & gratitude I give
For this beautiful life I get to live.

BLISS

I still meditate every day, and I'm a vegetarian now. I know the things I need to do to take care of myself. I still practice reiki, but just on myself for the time being.

My journey throughout this lifetime continues, I embrace each day with excitement, not knowing what I'm going to learn or what is going to unfold. My heart is fully open. I feel everything so much more deeply. Not only love, but I also feel pain more deeply too. I would rather feel than to have a wall built up around me again.

The past eight years have involved a major transformation not only for me but for Ash as well. I am so thankful for who I am today, for all the beauty that I get to see, and for all the love that surrounds me.

It's funny how the years seem to fly by. It feels like suddenly you look in the mirror and you see yourself and think, *Wow is that me? Where have the years gone?* I have these moments often, but I always smile back now, because I love the person who is looking back at me. In fully loving myself, I can also love others so much more.

Ash and I have now been married for thirty years, and I know that the connection that I have with Ash is at a soul level or we would never have made it through our hardships. We are both continually growing and expanding as a couple, and we both love each other unconditionally for who we truly are. I was sincerely blessed the day that Ash came into my life. His unconditional love has helped me shed the layers and break through the walls that I had put up.

Who I am today is the real me, the whole me, the me that has no walls or pretence. The me that shines from an open heart that is full of love to give.

I believe that every experience that we have is an opportunity to work through, heal, and expand into who we truly are. I believe that everyone here on this beautiful planet is also on a journey: a journey back to their true state, and that true state is love.

With Love

On the following pages are some recommendations for cleansing techniques, spiritual books, uplifting music, and other information that I would like to share with you.

I believe that when we are truly happy with who we are, and we are in the flow of life, then love and happiness cannot help but overflow through every part of our lives, including going to those who are around us.

I wish you all love and happiness.

Tanya x

Heaven shines upon the forest floor,
Webs float in the breeze.

Birds sing their morning songs,
Dew drops sparkle on the leaves.

In awe I stand, taking everything in,
Feeling open & connected to all life.

Thanks I give to Mother Nature
For opening my heart & eyes.

What Helps Me

Control

It helps me to know that I cannot control another person's reaction to what I'm saying when I speak my truth. If there is a reaction that isn't that great, then it's their stuff to work through and not mine.

Gratitude

I give thanks every day for something that I appreciate. Often I give thanks throughout the day.

Fear

We can't let ourselves give into fear. It can cripple us and hold us back in so many ways. Looking back, that is exactly what happened to me.

Don't get me wrong, I still have moments when fear surfaces. One example has been in writing this book. In being open and honest about being an empath (one who feels others' emotions), fear is coming up for me; the fear of what people might think. But to speak my truth is liberating and freeing, to say the least. It is none of my concern what people think or say about me. What is my concern is that I am my true, authentic self and that I speak my truth.

Spiritual texts

I love reading spiritual books. The knowledge that is held within such books has helped me to expand and grow throughout my spiritual journey. On the pages to come, I have listed some books that I recommend.

Unattachment from outcome

Right now, I am focusing on the words that are flowing through me onto these pages instead of being worried about the end result or how well the book will sell. I am enjoying every moment that I write, and I'll leave the rest to the universe. In doing this, I have the full enjoyment of being in the present moment.

Inner guidance

It has taken me many years to start listening to my inner guidance. For so long, I ignored my body and how things made me feel. Instead, I was busy trying to escape. As soon as I started to listen, my energy lifted even more.

Only you know what is right for you. You are the one who knows how you are feeling inside. You have all you need within you, and you already know what feels right. Just be aware, shine bright, and don't let anyone dull your sparkle.

Intention

Having a clear intention keeps me centred and aligned with my belief system, (how I choose to live and what I believe in). An intention gives me a chance to go within and be clear about what I am going to do and why.

If my intention does not align with my belief system, I will not do it. For example, when I post my photographs on Facebook, I set a clear intention to help nature, to share Mother Nature's beauty and bring awareness to her.

Awareness

I take note each day of what I'm doing and how it is making me feel. The moment I started doing this and doing more of the things that made me feel good, my energy shifted. I felt so much better in myself.

Now, I only surround myself with people who make me feel good. If I do need to be around people who I find it hard to be around, I limit my time with them. I also visualise myself being flooded in a white and pink light and ask that only what is for my highest good passes through to me.

I only watch television shows that feel okay to watch—like a good comedy—and I only eat food that energises me.

Being aware of my breath also brings an instant awareness to me. I notice if my breath is shallow in my chest or if it is a deep breath to the belly. Watching my breath brings my attention to what is happening within me and shifts my focus away from the mind chatter.

Being alone in nature

I treasure my alone time. It allows me to just be, to listen, and to feel what is going on within me. Time to reconnect with myself.

I am very grateful for where I live. Our property backs onto native bushland, and I love spending time bushwalking, just wandering through the trees and listening to the local wildlife and sitting if I feel the need.

Clean living

The food I eat is homegrown and free of chemicals. It's amazing how much better it tastes and how much better it is for you. I choose to live cleanly, which also helps to lift my energy levels.

Journaling

Getting what I am feeling out onto paper has helped me so much through the years. I always finish my journaling with a list of things that I am grateful for. This has helped to keep me focused on all the beauty and love in my life.

We bring into our lives what we focus on. It's true that where the attention goes, the energy flows. That's why I choose to focus on all the wonderful things in my life. I appreciate every moment I have on this beautiful planet—even the moments that aren't so great and that I may not appreciate at the time. I believe those moments give us a chance to grow and expand, to look at why we reacted that way, and to see what we can learn.

Salt baths

I have regular salt baths and salt foot baths to clear my aura and remove toxins. I also meditate with a small bowl of salt in front of me to clear my aura when I feel the need to.

Balance

I am aware how important it is for me to have balance in my life. If I have a lot of computer work or paperwork to do, I balance it with being in nature. If I'm feeling tired, I rest. If I'm feeling energised, I'll flow with that also.

Prayer

I remember when I was a little girl, my mum taught me a prayer to say every night before I went to sleep. I still sometimes say that prayer now.

*Dear Lord, thank you for my happy day.
Forgive any wrong thing that I have done.
Watch over me while I sleep tonight
and bless everyone I love. Amen.*

Another prayer that I love is to ask that my family and friends are flooded in love, light and happiness. It's simple but meaningful to me.

Calm surrounds

My home is filled with lots of laughter and love. I choose to live in peace, so my home is also a peaceful place. As I cleared out all the stored emotions inside me, I also cleared out my home. I slowly spring-cleaned every room in my home over the years and painted most of the dark furniture white to lighten up my space.

Colour

I used to wear mostly black clothing, but now I wear so many bright colours that when I walk past a mirror and catch a glimpse of myself, I giggle and smile. Bright colours make me happy. I also love having colourful flowers throughout my home to brighten things up.

Removing toxins from my life

I have found that the more energetically open I became, the more sensitive I became to outside influences too. I'm allergic to Teflon, so all cookware in the house got changed to cast iron. I also need to limit time I spend on the computer due to the electromagnetic field.

It's amazing how when you start really looking at what things are made of (including food, clothing and household items), you begin to find out what substances have been added to these items that are harmful to us.

I take activated charcoal at least once a month to clean out any toxins that have built up in my system. It is important to listen to how you are feeling, though. If I feel that I don't need the charcoal, I won't take it.

Singing bowls

I love playing my singing bowls, and I normally open and close my meditation with them. They help to cleanse my aura and lift my vibration.

Crystals

I have a deep love for crystals, letting my inner guidance determine which crystal I will wear for the day.

FIND OUT WHAT WORKS FOR YOU

Cleansing Techniques

Chakra shower

You can either stand or sit for this practice. Visualise a beautiful white and pink light (or any colours you are guided to use) flowing through your chakras. Start with your soul star, which is located 15 centimetres above your crown chakra, then move through all your other chakras. Let the light flow all the way down to your earth star, which is located 30 to 45 centimetres below the soles of your feet.

As you visualise this beautiful energy flowing through you, know that it purifies and clears your chakras and aura, then fills you up with beautiful divine love and light.

Grounding

If I'm needing a quick energetic pick-me-up, I'll stand on the grass to ground myself. I will ask Mother Earth for her help in cleansing and energising me. Or I will sit under a tree for a while with my feet on the ground. I do this especially if I have spent a lot of time on the computer.

Chanting

I have found chakra chanting to be an effective and enjoyable way to clear and align my chakras. While chanting, I visualise the colour of the chakra that I am clearing and aligning.

I use chakra chanting in two ways. The first is at the end of a meditation, to clear and align any chakras that I feel need attention. The second is in a meditation totally dedicated to chakra chanting.

For this type of chanting, I start at the base chakra and work my way up through all the chakras. You can hear the chakras become clear while doing this practice, so you will know within yourself when to move on to the next one. After completing this process, I always feel centred, aligned, peaceful, and clear.

The table below shows the sound to chant for each chakra, along with the colour associated with that chakra:

Sound	Pronounced	Chakra	Colour
LAM	LLUUMM	Base	Red
VAM	VVUUMM	Sacral	Orange
RAM	RRUUMM	Solar plexus	Yellow
YAM	YYUUMM	Heart	Pink or green
HAM	HHUUMM	Throat	Blue
OM	OOMM	Third eye	Indigo
AUM	AAUUMM	Crown	Violet

Quite often when I spend time in the bush, I will quietly start chanting *Aum*, gradually getting louder and louder until I'm chanting at the top of my lungs with my throat chakra totally clear and open. The first time I did this, I giggled to myself when I finished. It was beautiful, chanting among the trees. Very liberating and freeing.

Quotes I Love

It is better to be hated for what you are, than be loved for what you are not.

-André Gide

Your task is not to seek for love, but merely to seek and find all the barriers within yourself that you have built against it.

-Rumi

If you truly loved yourself, you could never hurt another.
-Buddha

For a flower to fully bloom, it must first open its heart centre and embrace the warmth of the sun.

-Tanya Gates

Goodbyes are only for those who love with their eyes. Because for those who love with heart and soul there is no such thing as separation.

-Rumi

Affirmations That Help Me

I am love
I am joy
I am happiness

I am abundant in everyway

I am one with nature

I am healed and whole
I am love
I am light
I am divine

I am balanced and aligned with my higher self

I am aligned with divine love

I choose love today

SPIRITUAL BOOKS THAT I RECOMMEND

Being in Balance: 9 Principles for Creating Habits to Match Your Desires by Dr Wayne W. Dyer

The Power of Now: A Guide to Spiritual Enlightenment by Eckhart Tolle

Falling into Grace: Insights on the End of Suffering by Adyashanti

A Return to Love: Reflections on the Principles of A Course in Miracles by Marianne Williamson

The Untethered Soul: The Journey Beyond Yourself by Michael A. Singer

Raise Your Vibration: 111 Practices to Increase Your Spiritual Connection by Kyle Gray

Light is the New Black: A Guide to Answering Your Soul's Callings and Working Your Light by Rebecca Campbell

The Seat of the Soul by Gary Zukav

Music That Uplifts Me

'Break the Shell' by India Arie

'In Dreams' by Jai-Jagdeesh

'Gayatri Mantra' by Deva Premal

'Peace' by Ajeet Kaur

'Return to Innocence' by Enigma

Acknowledgements

All of my poems in this book are dedicated to Mother Nature, with love and gratitude for the many hours of treasured moments you have shared with me.

I send love to all the beautiful souls that have come into my life. They have shared their unconditional love with me which has guided me along this amazing journey called life.

I give thanks to my husband, Ash, and my beautiful children and grandchildren, who fill my life with such joy and happiness that it makes my heart sing each and every day.

I give thanks to all the great masters who have shared their wisdom with me through their spiritual texts.

I give thanks for all the guidance and healing that flowed through me while I was writing the chapters in this book.

For the Love of My Life

The love you have given me has helped to set me free,
Now I truly embrace who I am meant to be

Over the years I have changed & grown,
But my heart has always been yours & yours alone

Heaven smiled upon me the day we were brought together;
I have found my soul mate & will be with you forever.

Love Always Tanya x

www.ingramcontent.com/pod-product-compliance
Lightning Source LLC
Chambersburg PA
CBHW071004080526
44587CB00015B/2346